First published in Great Britain in 2000 by
David & Charles Children's Books,
Winchester House, 259-269 Old Marylebone Road, London NW1 5XJ

Text © Adèle Geras 2000
Illustrations © Emma Chichester Clark 2000

ISBN: 1 86233 231 2

A CIP catalogue record for this title is available from the British Library.

Printed and bound in Belgium

The Magic of the Ballet

Swan Lake

RETOLD BY ADÈLE GERAS

ILLUSTRATED BY EMMA CHICHESTER CLARK

David & Charles
Children's Books

The Magic of the Ballet

HUMAN BEINGS LIKE TO move their bodies in time to rhythm. Even the tiniest babies enjoy being rocked or gently bounced as you sing to them, and we all know how feet long to move when we hear a strong and exciting beat. "That's toe-tapping music," we say, and what we mean is we would like to dance to it.

There are many different kinds of dance: folk, disco, ballroom, tap and so on.

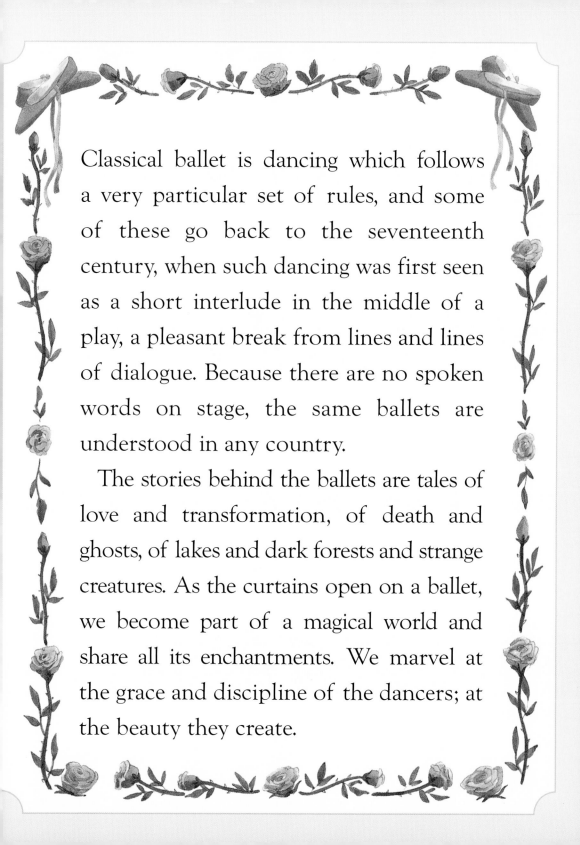

Classical ballet is dancing which follows a very particular set of rules, and some of these go back to the seventeenth century, when such dancing was first seen as a short interlude in the middle of a play, a pleasant break from lines and lines of dialogue. Because there are no spoken words on stage, the same ballets are understood in any country.

The stories behind the ballets are tales of love and transformation, of death and ghosts, of lakes and dark forests and strange creatures. As the curtains open on a ballet, we become part of a magical world and share all its enchantments. We marvel at the grace and discipline of the dancers; at the beauty they create.

'Von Rothbart swooped down from his branch and the black span of his wings obscured the moon.'

Swan Lake

LISTEN. THESE THINGS HAPPENED long ago. There was daylight and darkness. There was Good and Evil. There was the kingdom and the forest. In the kingdom, Prince Siegfried was about to celebrate his birthday. The forest, however, was the lair of the magician, Von Rothbart.

In the deepest and greenest part of the forest, there was a silver lake which people called 'The Lake of Swans'. Whispers were that every bird floating on the still waters was really a young maiden trapped by Von Rothbart and transformed into a swan for as long as there was light in the sky.

At dusk, (so the story went) each bird took on her human shape for the length of the night, and in this way, Von Rothbart would remind them of the human happiness they had lost. Every single night, the magician took on the feathers and talons and wide amber eyes of an enormous owl, and he sat and watched the pale dancers from the branches of a tree beside the lake. The most magnificent swan of all was once a princess. As the sun set, and her feathered wings fluttered into arms, she would remember her name.

"I was Odette," she would sigh. "Once, I was Odette."

But listen. It was the day of Prince Siegfried's birthday, and in the palace, everyone was preparing for the celebrations.

The Queen had planned a ball, and every eligible young lady from every neighbouring country had been invited.

"It is time," the Queen told her son, "that you found yourself a wife. There is a limit to the time a young man of royal birth should spend in frivolous pursuits such as hunting."

"Then why, dearest Mother, did you present me with this crossbow as a birthday gift?" replied the Prince.

"Because I knew it would please you," said the Queen. "In return, I insist that you please me and choose a wife at the ball tomorrow night."

"Very well, Mother," said Prince Siegfried. "You know I would do anything to bring a smile to your lips. Until the ball,

however, I am a free man and I'll enjoy my 'frivolous pursuits', as you call them, for a little while longer."

Siegfried looked out of the window, thinking that perhaps it was too late to go hunting that day. Just then, however, a formation of white swans crossed the sky, making for the dense forest.

"Come," Siegfried called to his companions, "we may be too late, but how beautiful they are! Let's follow them."

The hunting party set off. Although the young men had heard stories about the foolishness of wandering through the forest at dusk, they put them out of their minds. Were they not armed? And what royal prince would ever admit that he was afraid? Nevertheless, as the shadows

thickened and the sky grew dark, Prince Siegfried's friends urged him to return to the safety of the palace.

"Wait," said Siegfried. "Can you see something white moving through the branches? I'm going to look."

He arrived at the clearing beside the lake in time to watch the great, white birds that he had been hunting fly down to the ground. He raised his crossbow to his

shoulder and aimed it at the most splendid swan of all, when suddenly, in a shudder of white light, the wings bent themselves into arms, the pale feathers were gone, and his arrow was pointed at the loveliest woman he had ever seen. The other birds had also turned into young maidens, but Siegfried threw down his bow and ran towards the one he already knew he would love forever.

"Please," he implored, as she tried to escape him. "Please, I will never hurt you, I promise. Please do not run from me."

In his nearby tree, Von Rothbart, in the guise of an owl, hooted and spread his dark wings, but Siegfried had eyes and ears only for the woman before him.

When he caught up with her, she

trembled in his arms as though she were still a bird and he a hunter, but his kind words soothed her in the end, and she spoke her name aloud to him.

"I am the Princess Odette," she said, "and I am condemned to be a swan during the daylight hours. We are all of us in Von Rothbart's power, and at night we dance in human form, but he watches us always. Even now, his eyes are fixed on us."

"Where?" cried Siegfried. "Show him to me and I will put a single arrow through his heart."

"Oh, no, you must not," cried Odette, "for then you will surely kill me! He has bound his life to mine and twisted them together in a single thread. If he dies, then so do I. The spell will be broken only

when I can find the person who will love me forever. Someone who will be faithful to me alone."

"Then you are free," Siegfried laughed, "for I shall love you through this life and beyond it. Come with me and be my bride."

Hearing these words, Von Rothbart swooped down from his branch and the black span of his wings obscured the moon. He clawed Odette to his side.

"Go!" said Odette. "There is nothing you can do. The dawn is nearly here and we shall all be swans again."

"I will come back for you," Siegfried cried. "I will find a way to break the spell."

"But go now," Odette sighed. "Only your faithful love can free me from this terror."

All through the next day, the day of the ball, Siegfried was in a dream of love and sorrow. How could he tell his mother that he had found his bride? How could he bring Odette to the palace when Von Rothbart watched and watched her with his amber eyes?

When the ball began, and all the princesses were paraded before him, Siegfried hardly noticed them. Then there came a knocking at the gates.

"Lady," said a messenger, kneeling before the Queen, "a knight and his daughter have arrived and they beg to enter."

"Let them in," said the Queen. "All are welcome at this feast."

The knight was dressed from head to foot in black. Something about his face, and the yellowish light that shone from his eyes seemed familiar to Siegfried, but then he caught sight of the knight's daughter, and recognized Odette, dressed in glittering black. So happy was he to see his swan-lady again that he forgot every other thought in his head and never considered how his beloved had come to be here, at the palace.

All through his life, the Prince had learned nothing about deception. Even the

presence of the black knight did not arouse his suspicions, but the Princess, although she had the body and face of Odette, was none other than Odile, Von Rothbart's daughter. Her father had given her the outward appearance of Odette for one reason and one reason alone: to entrance and delude poor Prince Siegfried, who would thus be tricked into breaking his faith with his true love.

And oh, this Odile, how she danced and turned, and turned and smiled and how

soft were the fires that shone from her eyes, binding Siegfried's heart to her, and pushing out of his mind every lingering memory of the real Odette's white dress and her gentle beauty.

They danced together in the light of a thousand candles, but Von Rothbart was always near, weaving stronger and stronger enchantment around them. And as they danced, at the high windows of the Great Hall there was a movement . . . a tremble of white at the glass, but no one saw it, and no one heard the frantic arms beating against the pane.

Von Rothbart spoke at last to Siegfried. "If you will promise to love my daughter forever, she shall be yours."

And the Prince (but where, where had he

seen eyes like that before, and why did the knight's black cloak remind him of wings?) spoke the words Von Rothbart was waiting to hear.

"I shall love her, and no one else, for the rest of my days. She is the bride that I have chosen."

A terrible cry came from somewhere high up. Prince Siegfried glanced at the window, and saw the bird-shape of Odette pushing at the glass: desperate, despairing.

The instant he looked back at the knight in black, he knew him to be Von Rothbart. And the young woman at his side? How could he, even for a single moment, have thought that she was his princess? And how could he save Odette,

now that he had broken his promise to her? Siegfried fled from the Great Hall and ran out into the night. He had to find Odette at the lake, and convince her of his love.

At the palace, the guests hurried to leave the ball. The candles flickered and guttered into darkness, and Von Rothbart and his daughter vanished into the night.

Beside the lake, Prince Siegfried found

his princess, weeping and heartbroken. Over and over again he pleaded with her: "I thought that she was you. Oh, the wickedness of that cursed magician!"

"The spell will never be broken for me now," said Odette, "but if I die, then he dies too. Our lives, his and mine, are twisted into a single thread. What can I live for now?"

"If you are gone," said Siegfried, "life has no meaning for me."

"Then let us die together," said Odette.

At that moment, black wings covered the moon, and Von Rothbart swooped down, desperately trying to pull Odette away from Siegfried.

Siegfried and Von Rothbart struggled and fought, and at last the Prince broke free of the talons and the beak. Taking Odette's hand, he ran towards the lake. A wind had sprung up, whipping the water into waves and whirlpools. The lovers flung themselves in, sinking deeper and deeper until all became silent and calm once again. Von Rothbart flew into the green heart of the forest to die.

Now the swan maidens were free but they wept bitterly for their princess and her love, together at last.

Listen. These things happened long ago. There is a lake in the forest to this day, but the swans are real swans now. Love, which is stronger than death and lasts forever, has destroyed an evil magic.

On nights when the moon is full, some say they have seen shadows that could be the Princess Odette and her prince, dancing beside the silver water of a lake. A lake they call the Lake of Swans.

SWAN LAKE WAS FIRST produced in 1877. The music was by Tchaikovsky, and the production was a failure. In 1894, after the composer's death, the ballet was revived with new choreography by Marius Petipa, and was a great success. Today, it is probably the best-known of all ballets.

Although you will often hear of daring experiments with plays – of Hamlet set in a prison, or Romeo and Juliet on the streets of New York – it is rarer for a ballet to be staged in a non-traditional way, although this is sometimes done.

There are, of course, many modern ballets which take place not in a sort of fairyland but in the real, recognizable world. *The Judas Tree*, for instance, takes place on a building site.

It is possible for classical ballets to be staged in different kinds of spaces: in the round, in school halls, in tents and so forth. But ballet companies have their homes, for the most part, in beautiful theatres which date back to the last century or earlier.

The Paris Opéra, right in the heart of the city, is a magnificent building. Inside, there are wide staircases, marble columns and all the glitter and glamour that we have come to associate with the ballet. The Maryinski Theatre in St Petersburg, the Bolshoi Theatre in Moscow, and

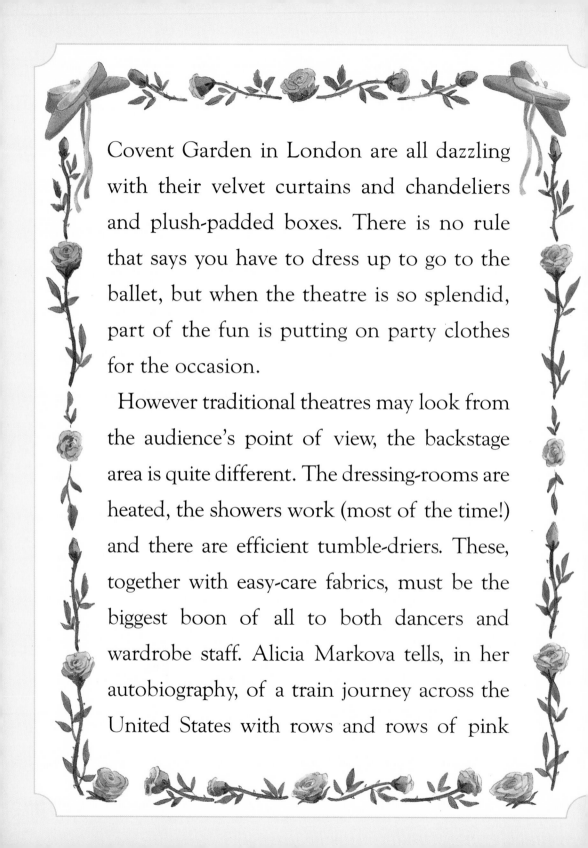

Covent Garden in London are all dazzling with their velvet curtains and chandeliers and plush-padded boxes. There is no rule that says you have to dress up to go to the ballet, but when the theatre is so splendid, part of the fun is putting on party clothes for the occasion.

However traditional theatres may look from the audience's point of view, the backstage area is quite different. The dressing-rooms are heated, the showers work (most of the time!) and there are efficient tumble-driers. These, together with easy-care fabrics, must be the biggest boon of all to both dancers and wardrobe staff. Alicia Markova tells, in her autobiography, of a train journey across the United States with rows and rows of pink cotton tights hung up to dry on a string stretched across the whole compartment. If she was lucky, they would be wearable before the next performance – if not, she would have to dance in damp tights!

The magic we see on stage is a combination of many elements. As the auditorium grows dark and the orchestra starts to play, we step into the dancers' imaginary world of music, drama and bright lights.

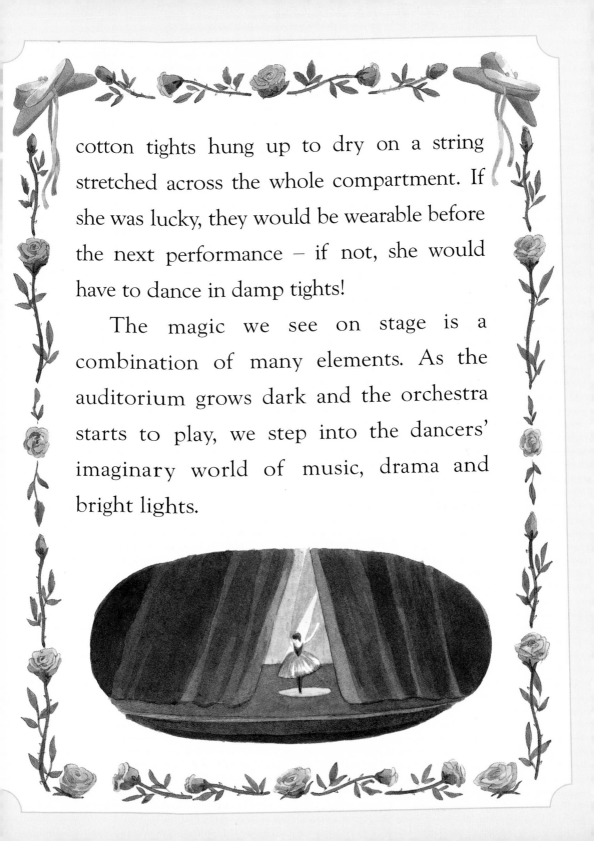

j398.209 Geras, Adele.
J
4
G   Swan Lake.

$10.95

DATE			

BAKER & TAYLOR